Caring for the Earth

RACHEL CARSON

by Elizabeth Ring

A Gateway Green Biography
The Millbrook Press
Brookfield, Connecticut

For Helen

Cover photograph courtesy of Alfred Eisenstaedt,
Life Magazine © Time Warner, Inc.
Background cover photograph courtesy of Superstock

Photographs courtesy of: Alfred Eisenstaedt, *Life*
Magazine © Time Warner, Inc. : p. 4; Rachel Carson
Council: pp. 8 (both), 10 (top), 16, 29, 30 (photo
by Shirley A. Briggs), 36 (photo by Shirley A. Briggs);
Beinecke Rare Book Library, Yale University: pp. 10
(bottom), 13 (top); Peter Arnold: pp. 13 (bottom) 24,
33 (both), 36 (top); Chatham College Archives, Jenny
Mellon Library, Pittsburgh, Pa.: p. 21 (both); Erich
Hartmann © Magnum Photos: p. 39 (top); AP/Wide
World Photos: p. 39 (bottom); Reuters/Bettman: p. 42.

Library of Congress Cataloging-in-Publication Data

Ring, Elizabeth, 1920-
Rachel Carson : caring for the earth / by Elizabeth Ring.

p.   cm. — (A Gateway green biography)
Includes bibliographical references and index.
Summary: A biography of the biologist, focusing on her
childhood in Pennsylvania, her growing interest as an adult
in environmental concerns, and the importance of her book
"Silent Spring" in exposing the environmental harm done
by pesticides.
ISBN 0-395-64730-4 (pbk.)
1. Carson, Rachel, 1907-1964—Juvenile literature.
2. Biologists—United States—Biography—Juvenile literature.
3. Environmentalists—United States—Biography—Juvenile
literature. 4. Science writers—United States—Biography—
Juvenile literature. [1. Carson, Rachel, 1907-1964.
2. Conservationists. 3. Biologists. 4. Science writers.]
I. Title. II. Series.
QH31.C33R56   1992
574'.092—dc20
[B]   91-37644   CIP   AC

Rachel Carson

Rachel Carson was always interested in the sea and everything that lived in and around it. Here, she takes a close look at a bunch of seaweed.

What if you lived in a pretty little town somewhere in the middle of America? (Maybe you do.) In your town there are tall, leafy trees and bright flower gardens. It is a place where you and your friends play ball in the park. Outside town, you go down country roads past farms and fields. You and your family often picnic down by the stream. It is a happy place to live.

Now, what if some mysterious evil spell fell on your town? The leaves on trees suddenly turned ugly brown. Flowers drooped. Dogs, cats, cows, and horses got sick. Some died. People got sick too. Fish vanished from the stream, which had turned dirty brown. And no birds sang. Only a deep, deadly silence hung in the air.

You would be scared. You would surely wonder: *What's going on here?* You'd want to do something to get your town back the way it used to be: clean and green—and alive.

Rachel Carson told a story about just such a town. She told the story to make people think. She was a biologist. She knew how plants and animals live. And she had found out what could cause plants and animals to die unnatural deaths like those she described.

Rachel Carson was not just imagining when she pictured a "silent spring." She had discovered that, without knowing it, people were in danger of destroying their world and themselves. They were using lots of chemical sprays and powders to kill pests, such as mosquitoes and weeds. But these pesticides were quickly spreading far and wide. They were poisoning the air, the water, the land, the plants and animals—and the people.

Rachel knew that something had to be done to wake people up. So she wrote a book she called *Silent Spring.* She started the book with the story of the little town, as a warning. Then she went on to tell how pesticides work and why they must be used very, very carefully.

Her book did just what she hoped. It scared people. It helped change the way many people thought about their world. It made many people try to treat their world better.

But this is not where Rachel Carson's story begins. By the time she wrote *Silent Spring,* she was already a famous writer and scientist.

Rachel Carson's story begins on a farm in Pennsylvania, back in 1907. It was spring in the small town of Springdale. It was the liveliest time of year. There on the farm, many new lives were beginning. There were new chicks and calves, piglets and rabbits. Baby birds were cheeping in nests. New buds were bursting out on bushes and trees.

And, on May 27, a new baby girl arrived at the Carsons' home. She was named Rachel Louise. The whole family thought this tiny child was quite special, and she was—as it turned out.

The Carsons lived the way many country people lived in those days. They drew their water from a well, and they grew much of their own food. Their "bathroom" was out back in a small shed called an outhouse. They drove into town by horse and buggy.

In her warm family circle, Rachel grew to be a bright, happy little girl. She was a bit shy, but she had a mind of her own. Her hazel eyes did not miss much that was going on. She found much to learn and to love. And she often found something to chuckle about, such as the time her little dog

Baby Rachel Louise Carson, held by her sister Marian.

Rachel's childhood was spent on a Pennsylvania farm. In this photo, she is seen with her mother, sister, and brother.

Candy tried to ride piggyback on a pig and kept sliding off! For a little while, the farm and her family were Rachel's whole world.

Her father, Robert, was not the kind of farmer who plowed fields and planted acres of corn or hay, as many Pennsylvania farmers did. Actually, he had bought the farm expecting to sell it off in small lots someday. He hoped to get rich that way. But that never happened.

Mr. Carson worked for a power company in town. He did not earn a great deal of money. Rachel grew up well cared for, but she also knew what it meant to work hard and to save.

There were two other Carson children. Rachel's sister Marian was ten when Rachel was born. Her brother Robert was eight. Of course, all the time Rachel was growing up, her brother and sister were "the big kids" and she was "the baby." That did not bother her a bit. Sometimes she tagged along after them. Many times the whole family gathered around the piano to sing songs. Often Rachel happily went her own way.

The most important person in Rachel's small world was her mother, Maria. Mrs. Carson was a

Rachel loved books
and animals. In this
picture she reads to
her dog, Candy.

Rachel (at center)
after a swim in
the river with her
brother, Robert,
and sister, Marian.

talented woman. She was a minister's daughter. She had gone to college at a time when not many girls did. She had been a music teacher before she married Rachel's father. Now her job as home-maker and mother kept her close to the farm.

Mrs. Carson and Rachel were very much alike. Nothing pleased either of them more than reading stories or going for walks through the woods and fields. They both loved all kinds of animals. Luckily, there were all those chickens and pigs, cows and horses, dogs and cats on the farm.

Long before Rachel went to school, her mother helped her explore the world they shared. The two of them spent hours outdoors. Sometimes they went outside very early in the morning, to listen to the birds' wake-up songs. What concerts they heard! Chirps and twitters, trills and squawks. And sometimes, like a drumbeat, the woodpecker went "rat-a-tat-tat" on a tree nearby.

Sometimes they went out at night. If they were very quiet, they might spot a 'possum or a raccoon. Sometimes they would just stare at the stars or watch the moonlight shimmer on the stream. It was enough to make anyone wonder about all the magical things in the natural world. And Rachel did wonder—and ask questions.

Often Mrs. Carson could not answer all Rachel's questions. So she would find a book that would tell about mice (or geese or earthworms, or whatever). The house was always full of books. Rachel loved make-believe stories about animals, too. *The Tale of Peter Rabbit* was a great favorite of hers.

As Rachel grew a bit older, she and her mother wandered farther and farther from the little farmhouse. And Rachel's world grew bigger and bigger. Most of the farm's sixty-five acres were just as they had always been, wild and unspoiled.

As they wandered through woods and across fields, Mrs. Carson and Rachel would talk about the kinds of plants they saw, or the lives of little animals. Once in a while, they talked about things that had nothing at all to do with nature: coal mines and factories and steel mills. Many had been built around Pittsburgh, a big city near Springdale.

They both thought it was too bad that factories puffed dirty smoke into the air. The factories were making the nearby Allegheny River muddy and

Rachel and her mother shared a love of nature and often spent time exploring the woods.

In Pittsburgh, near the Carson home, steel mills like this puffed smoke into the air.

smelly, too. It was sad to see the land torn up to dig coal. Someone had once asked to dig mines in part of their farm. Mr. Carson had said no. Mrs. Carson hoped nothing like that would happen to their land.

Rachel hoped so, too. But, like her mother, she could see how there had to be mines and factories *somewhere*. How else would things get made? And factories made jobs for people. Didn't her own father work at the power plant? It would be nice, though, if factories could make things without spoiling the countryside so. Maybe someone would find the answer to problems like that, someday.

The Springdale Grammar School was Rachel's first world away from home. What discoveries she made there! Numbers helped you count apples and figure how long until your birthday. Words helped you make stories and poems.

In second grade, Rachel wrote a lot of poems. She made rhymes about such things as "a mouse in the house" and "a frog on a log." One day, she made a little book of her poems. She printed her father's name on it and gave it to him. She even drew pictures of birds and animals to go with the words. Rachel felt very happy when her little book made a big hit with the family.

A couple of years later, in 1917, when Rachel was in the fourth grade, World War I was being fought in Europe. Rachel was learning about the war at school. It seemed far away. Then Robert, who had joined the air force, told his family about a brave aviator he knew of. This daring airman had saved his plane by crawling out on a damaged wing to balance the plane until his flying partner safely landed it. Robert's tale made the war seem more real.

Rachel wrote about the aviator's adventure. She sent her story to *St. Nicholas,* a magazine that many children loved to read at that time. In a special section, the magazine published stories written by children. Not only did *St. Nicholas* print her story, they paid her ten dollars for it and gave her a silver badge. After that, the magazine printed two other stories she wrote.

By the time Rachel was in the fifth grade, she was saying that she thought she would be a writer

Rachel (at left) with Robert, in his air force uniform, and Marian. When Rachel was a fourth grader, she wrote a story about a daring airman based on a tale her brother had told her.

16

when she grew up. Her friends cheered her on. Rachel had made some good friends at school, especially Mildred, Irene, and Charlotte. They all loved to read and go walking. Mildred, like Rachel, wrote poems.

Good company was wonderful, and there were lots of fun times. But Rachel liked to be alone, too. Doing quiet things suited her. And besides, it was when she was quiet and alone that she most often got to wondering about things, such as how ants live in anthills or how caterpillars make cocoons.

One spring morning, Rachel was up and outdoors alone. She wanted to have some time to herself before school. It was a beautiful day, and Rachel ran down to the stream. She took off her shoes and socks. She hitched up her skirt and waded into the cold, tumbling water, right up to her knees. The cold made her toes tingle. It felt great! She just stood there with her eyes closed and smiled to herself.

Many times in her life, it would seem to Rachel as if she were somehow connected to the whole world. That morning was probably like many others. It's easy to imagine her there—the stream pulling at her bare legs, branches nodding over her head, a breeze stirring her hair. She often felt that when birds sang, it was as if they were speaking to *her.* How wonderful to be part of the life that was swirling around her!

Perhaps this was one of the many times when Rachel wondered what it would feel like to stand at the edge of the ocean.

She had been reading a lot about the sea. And, once, when she held a conch shell to her ear, she thought she heard the sound of waves on the shore. She dreamed of going, someday, far away from Springdale, to the sea. But that would not happen for a few more years.

After finishing Springdale Grammar School, Rachel spent two years at Springdale High. Then, for two more years, she went to Parnassus High, another high school nearby.

Each change of schools meant a change in Rachel's world. There were new places to explore and new people to know. And, especially, there were new things to learn.

Not many of her classmates liked books and classes as much as Rachel did. But Rachel was never a bore, her friends said. She never bragged about her high grades either.

Everyone liked Rachel's writing. She always had such good ideas. She said things so well.

With high hopes for becoming "a real writer," Rachel went on to Pennsylvania College for Women (later called Chatham College), in Pittsburgh. It was 1925 and World War I was over. It seemed as if almost everyone in America wanted to put those bad war years behind them. They wanted to have some fun.

At college, Rachel found herself in a world full of parties and dances. Rachel liked good times, but her classes were more important to her than parties. For one thing, she did not have as much money to spend as many of the other girls. She couldn't buy lots of party dresses and dancing shoes. She couldn't even pay for ice-cream sodas very often. It was hard enough for her parents to pay for her to be at college at all. Besides, she knew she had to do her very best if she was to learn all she wanted to know.

So Rachel worked hard. Now, as always, she went her own friendly way. Of course, she did not have her nose buried in books *all* the time. She played field hockey. She even helped win some games. She played the violin too. In winter, she sometimes went sledding with her friends. In summer, there were picnics to share. Those things did not cost money. She saved up for special good times. When she went to her prom, she wore new silver shoes.

All through college, Rachel's writing got better and better. She was a reporter for the college newspaper. She wrote for the college magazine, too. By the end of her second year, she had won the English Club prize.

That same year, Rachel made a big discovery. It opened up a really exciting new world for her. She started taking biology, the science of living things. Biology explained so much about things she had wondered about: why leaves are green, how oysters built their shells, things like that. She learned, too, of the "web of life" that links all living things. She had already guessed that. She thought of the many times she had felt as if she were really

This photograph of Rachel Carson was taken during her college days.

Rachel (back row, second from right), poses with her college field-hockey team.

connected to everything around her—woven, as it were, into the great "web of life."

Before long, she had decided to be a scientist. Rachel's friends and her English teacher were amazed. They told her she would have more success in life as a writer than as a scientist.

But the science bug had bitten Rachel hard. Maybe deep in her heart she hoped she could be a biologist and a writer, too. She kept on writing.

As it turned out, she *could* be both. All the books she later wrote tell wonderful stories. Sometimes the words sound like beautiful poems. At the same time, the books are chock-full of facts about nature. Rachel Carson's books make science come truly alive. Few other books had done that before.

On *a lovely May day* in 1929, Rachel Carson finished college. It was spring again, her favorite time of year. Once more, it was that season for new beginnings. She was more than ready to step into her next world. Imagine! She was going to Woods Hole on Cape Cod, on the Massachusetts coast. At last, she would see the Atlantic Ocean.

On her way there, she wondered if the sea would be all she had dreamed it would be.

Yes, it was—and more. Wading in the salt water was even better than wading in the stream back home. She felt the tide pull at her bare legs and the sand sink under her toes. She closed her eyes. Gusts of salt air sent her hair flying. She smelled the seaweed on the beach. She listened to the waves lap the shore and the gulls screech overhead. Louder than ever, nature was speaking to *her.*

That summer at Woods Hole, Rachel Carson worked and studied at the Marine Biological Laboratory, a place where many scientists were studying sea life.

The longer she lived by the sea, the more she found herself staring out over the water and wondering things like: *What is going on beneath those rolling waves? How would it feel to live like a fish?*

That fall, she went to Johns Hopkins, a university in Baltimore, Maryland. Her good grades at her first college had won her a full scholarship. That meant it would cost her very little to study more about the life of the sea. She had no idea how hard the next few years were going to be for her.

*Woods Hole Marine Biological Laboratory
in Massachusetts, as it appears today.*

The years that followed 1929 were hard ones for almost everyone in America. Those years were called the Great Depression. There were few jobs for anyone. Many people had barely enough money to live on. Both Rachel's father and brother had lost their jobs in Pennsylvania.

The Carson family asked one another how they could make the most of what little money they had. Rachel's parents finally decided to leave the farm and move in with Rachel. Sister Marian moved in, too, with her two little daughters. Even brother Robert was there for a while. They lived together in a house in the country, not far from Johns Hopkins.

Rachel's mother took care of the house and did the cooking. That was fine with Rachel, who hated to cook. Soon, Robert found work in Baltimore. He didn't earn much, but every cent helped. One day, Robert's "pay" was not money, but a Persian cat. He brought Mitzi home, and Rachel took to the silky-haired cat right away.

Besides going to classes, Rachel herself had two small jobs. She was a laboratory helper at Johns Hopkins. She also taught biology at the University of Maryland. She worked long, hard hours, often studying and writing late into the night.

Nighttime was a good time to write. The whole house was quiet. Everyone was asleep. She was alone. But she was not lonely. Not with Mitzi the cat purring beside her!

*R*achel Carson's studies at Johns Hopkins ended in 1932. She now had a master's degree in marine biology. That meant that she really knew a lot about the lives of sea creatures. But there were not many jobs for a biologist just then, especially if the biologist was a woman. She still had one small job at Johns Hopkins. And some summers she worked and studied at Woods Hole Marine Biological Laboratory on Cape Cod.

Then, in 1935, on a rainy July day, Rachel's father died. His sudden death was a terrible shock. The family mourned. But life had to go on. There was much work to do, many bills to pay. Soon Rachel was looking hard for a second job. She finally found one in Washington, D.C.

The day Carson walked into the United States

Bureau of Fisheries, she was, of course, looking for work as a marine biologist. She was told that what was really needed was someone to write radio programs about fish. Imagine her surprise when she was asked: "Can you write?"

Well, yes, as a matter of fact, she could.

That job let her prove that she could be both a scientist and a writer. Before long, she became an editor as well as a writer of nature stories and government reports. She was kept very busy at work.

She was busy at home, too. By 1936, she and her mother had Rachel's two little nieces to care for. Marian had died, and her daughters, Marjorie and Virginia, now shared a new home in Silver Spring, Maryland, with Rachel and her mother. The little girls went to grammar school there.

During this time, Carson started her first book. As she had done before, she wrote late into the night. Now she had the company of Buzzie and Kito, Mitzi's silky-haired offspring. The two purring cats curled up on her desk among her papers.

She named the book *Under the Sea Wind.* It was different from other books about the sea. In it, Carson makes you see sea life as if you are swimming alongside a fish or an eel or some other sea creature. She takes you to places in the ocean where people have never been, such as a deep, dark abyss, or pit.

In one part of the book, you meet a mackerel named Scomber. He is "a powerful fish, streamlined . . . and a rover of the seas." Scomber has many narrow escapes. Once he is being chased by some tunas. He is almost caught when, suddenly, three killer whales attack the tunas. Scomber just barely gets away. You feel as if you are right there, fleeing with the swift mackerel.

Almost everybody who read the book liked *Under the Sea Wind.* But few copies of the book were sold. That was because, in 1941, Americans were caught up in World War II. They were too busy to read books about life in the sea.

Rachel Carson herself was busier than ever during the war, and after. By 1947, she was the editor in chief at the U.S. Fish and Wildlife Service.

All this time, she never stopped reading and studying and dreaming about the sea. She would find herself wondering: *How is the sea made? How deep is it? Where do ocean currents come from?*

Looking relaxed and happy, Rachel has fun trying her sunglasses on her dog outside her home in Maryland.

Diving helmet at her feet, Rachel sets out to explore the ocean.

The questions piled up. She went looking for answers. She even went out in a boat one day, put on a diving helmet and weighted boots, and dropped into 15 feet (4.5 meters) of water. Down there, it was at least *something* like seeing as a fish sees.

Then she started to write her new book. As she worked on it—at night, of course—she had the company of a new cat. This one was named Muffin and had a fine purr.

It took her three years to write *The Sea Around Us.* But when it was published, the name Rachel Carson became known all over the world.

Nobody had ever read a book like this. It is a sort of biography of the sea. Carson tells the ocean's life story—as if the sea were a person—from its beginnings, which "must have [been] more than 2 billion years ago."

She describes the sea's currents, tides, and waves, its mountains and valleys, and its plants and creatures. As in her first book, she makes the sea come alive.

"The deep sea has its stars," Carson tells us in one part. These are really lights in fishes' bodies.

The lights, she says, may help a hungry fish catch another to eat. No plants grow in the deep sea, so other fish are a fish's only food—except for the bits of dead and dying plants and animals that drift down from the sea's surface, like "a slow rain."

The Sea Around Us won many prizes. Then her first book, *Under the Sea Wind,* was published again. Now people had time to read it. Rachel Carson's fame spread.

Carson was happy that her books were well liked. But she didn't much care for all the attention people gave *her.* She had to go to dinners and receptions and other events given in her honor. She once told a friend, "I would much rather be barefoot in the sand . . . than on wood floors in high heels."

There was one very good thing about having written books lots of readers wanted to buy. Carson now had enough money to do the things that were most important to her. By the summer of 1952 she had left her job with the Fish and Wildlife Service. She had more books to write.

That summer she and her mother rented a home by the sea in Maine. And in 1953, she built a

This northern Red Sea anemone (right) and this American goose-fish (below) are among the creatures you might meet in places Rachel Carson described in her books.

cottage there, in West Southport. "I have my own shoreline and my own . . . woodland," she told a friend.

She was where she felt she was meant to be, at home beside the sea she loved and knew so much about.

Carson began a new book. She called this one *The Edge of the Sea.* This time she told the story of the seashore. It was about the creatures that live where the sea meets the land, where the tides come and go. Before she wrote it, she explored the Atlantic coast, from Maine to Florida.

Getting to know the shore, she wrote, means a lot more than walking on a beach and picking up shells. It means thinking about "the whole life of the creature that once inhabited the empty shell." It means asking questions like: How did the creature eat, sleep, and deal with its enemies?

The Edge of the Sea was published in 1955. It was another great success. Before this, few people had known much about ecology, the science of how plants and animals relate to each other and to the places in which they live. Each special place where an animal lives—such as a bog, a desert, the woods, or the seashore—is called a habitat. In order to survive, plants and animals need each other and the place where they live.

In her book, Carson shows how sandpipers and ghost crabs are at home on sandy beaches. She writes of the mussels and starfish that live in mossy tide pools on rocky coasts. And she tells about the animals called polyps that build coral reefs where bright-colored tropical fishes swim. She explains why these special places must be protected so that both creatures and plants can go on living where they belong.

Carson wrote parts of the book in her new cottage in Maine. But she also took time off to enjoy herself. With new friends and old, she went on picnics and sailboat rides. And, as always, there were walks with her mother. Some of the best times were when her niece Marjorie visited with her little son Roger.

Then, when Roger was five years old, Marjorie died. She had been ill for some time. Roger came to live with Rachel, and she adopted him as her

Rachel Carson
explores a tide pool
on the beach near
her home in Maine.

Starfish like these
were among the
treasures Rachel
found in tidepools.

own child. She often took Roger exploring—just as her mother had taken her when she was little.

Later, in a book called *A Sense of Wonder,* Rachel Carson tells about times she and Roger shared. They would roam the seashore and woodlands of Maine. Together, they found wood paths "carpeted with . . . a narrow strip of silvery gray" moss. After a rain, the moss was "deep and springy. Roger delighted in . . . getting down on chubby knees to feel it, and running from one patch to another to jump up and down in the deep . . . carpet with squeals of pleasure."

The year after Roger came to live with her, Carson began work on a new book. From the time she had known about the factories and mines around Pittsburgh, she had felt sad that things that help people also often spoil the air, land, and water—the environment—around them.

Then one day she heard from a friend that birds were dying where trees were being sprayed with a pesticide. The spray was a deadly pest-killer called DDT. Many people thought that saving trees from being destroyed by pests was a good, helpful thing for both the trees and people. The trouble was, the poison was spreading to other creatures, such as birds. That was surely a bad thing. Nobody knew where the poisoning would end. How much of the environment was already being spoiled?

Carson had long known about the dangers of pesticides. Now she began to read more about them and to ask more questions. The more she learned about pesticides, the more she saw that their use had to be carefully controlled.

Somebody had to let people know how dangerous poisonous chemicals are. That "somebody" turned out to be Rachel Carson herself.

During the four years she was writing *Silent Spring,* Carson was sick a good part of the time. Then her mother died. Between missing her mother and not feeling at all well, she wondered if she would ever finish her book. But she did. When Rachel Carson started a thing, she finished it. And she did it right.

Silent Spring was published in 1962. It was the most important of all the books Rachel Carson wrote. She became a pioneer, a leader of the envi-

With her grandnephew, Roger, Rachel examines a seashell on the beach.

A plane sprays DDT on sheep to kill ticks and fleas. Rachel Carson believed DDT could be deadly to all living things. She wrote about this in Silent Spring.

ronmental movement. After this time, people understood better how to work for pure air and for clean water and land.

In her book, Carson talked about the sprays and dusts that were applied "to farms, gardens, forests, and homes." These were "chemicals that have the power to kill every insect, the 'good' and the 'bad,' to still the song of birds and the leaping of fish in the streams, to coat the leaves with a deadly film, and to linger on in the soil." Then she asked: "Can anyone believe it is possible to lay down such . . . poisons on the surface of the earth without making it unfit for all life?"

Some people were shocked by *Silent Spring.* They wanted everyone to stop using pesticides right away. Other people—especially companies that made pesticides—were angry. They wanted Rachel Carson to stop her attack on pesticides right away. Some people thought she was crazy. They said she was making things up. But she was not.

In 1963, President John F. Kennedy spoke up for *Silent Spring.* That meant that the United States government would take up her fight.

By 1970, a special organization called the Environmental Protection Agency was set up. And in 1972, rules were made to ban the use of DDT. That was what she had hoped would happen.

How she would have applauded! But she didn't live to see that happen, or to see all the other good things that were done because of her work. She was awarded the Presidential Medal of Freedom after she died. Her picture was used on a U.S. postage stamp. A national wildlife refuge in Maine was named for her. And the Rachel Carson Council was formed to carry on the environmental work she had begun. But she never knew of these and many other honors that came along.

Rachel Carson had known since 1961 that she had cancer and did not have long to live. She died on April 14, 1964. It was spring again. To Rachel, spring had always meant beginnings, not endings. It is not hard to imagine that, that spring, she was wondering: *What comes next?*

What if *Rachel Carson* were still here today? Once she wrote: "I may not like what I see, but it does no good to ignore it." She would certainly

Children in Hong Kong celebrate Earth Day. Today many people are working to make this planet a better place.

be pleased to see so many groups of people who are *not* ignoring the world's environmental problems: the National Resources Defense Council, the National Wildlife Federation (which publishes *Ranger Rick's Nature Magazine*), the National Audubon Society, the Sierra Club, Greenpeace, and many others. She would be delighted that thousands of people celebrate Earth Day each spring.

What would Rachel Carson want to do about the environment we have created for ourselves?

She would surely be behind every effort to make the world a better place to live. She would want the rain forests and wetlands to be protected. She would want the dumping of garbage and poisonous toxic wastes to be controlled. She would want the chemicals that harm the air around us to be checked.

And what new worlds would Rachel Carson find to explore? Would she be trying to find new ways to recycle the throwaway things we use? What about new ways to feed the hungry? Would the mysteries of space excite her as much as the mysteries of the seas once had?

You really have to wonder!

Important Dates

1907	Born May 27 in Springdale, Pennsylvania.
1913	Goes to Springdale Grammar School.
1915–1918	Writes her first poems and stories.
1925	Finishes high school and enters Pennsylvania College for Women (Chatham College), where she discovers biology.
1929	Finishes college and goes to Cape Cod, where she gets her first view of the ocean.
1932	Earns a master's degree in marine biology from Johns Hopkins University.
1936	Joins the United States Bureau of Fisheries.
1941	*Under the Sea Wind* is published.
1951	*The Sea Around Us* is published.
1953	Builds a cottage on the seashore in Maine.
1955	*The Edge of the Sea* is published.
1962	*Silent Spring* is published.
1964	Dies April 14 in Silver Spring, Maryland.
1965	*A Sense of Wonder* is published.

Further Reading

About Rachel Carson

Rachel Carson: Biologist and Author, by Marty Jezer (Chelsea House, 1988).

Sounding the Alarm: A Biography of Rachel Carson, by Judith Harlan (Dillon Press, 1989).

About the environment

Chains, Webs & Pyramids, by Laurence Pringle (Crowell, 1975).

50 Simple Things Kids Can Do to Save the Earth, by the Earthworks Group (Andrews and McMeel, 1990).

The Future for the Environment, by Mark Lambert (Watts, 1986).

Life in the Sea, by Philip Steele (Watts, 1986).

Pollution, by Herta Breiter (Raintree Publishers, 1987).

See Along the Shore, by Millicent E. Selsam (Harper & Row, 1961).

By Rachel Carson

Under the Sea Wind (Simon and Schuster, 1941).

The Sea Around Us (Oxford University Press, 1951).

The Edge of the Sea (Houghton Mifflin, 1955).

Silent Spring (Houghton Mifflin, 1962).

The Sense of Wonder (Harper and Row, 1965).

Index